Pine Tree on Silk and a Yellow Linen Chair

A collection of poems by Laraine Kentridge Lasdon

Pine Tree on Silk and a Yellow Linen Chair

ISBN 979-8-218-34040-7

Contents

Journeys   1
Pine Tree On Silk And A Yellow Linen Chair   3
A Memory Of My Mother   5
Breathe With Me. Ubuntu   6
Dance Of The Crescent Moon   8
A Bird And The Hand   10
Again   12
Bat   14
Memory Fragments   16
A Hot Afternoon in Nice   18
Roses   20
Covenant Compass   22

This book is dedicated to my darling husband Leon and precious daughter Claire for their unwavering support

Journeys

The Book of Numbers is a counting and an
Accounting of people seeking peace
And a land to rest in. It is a recording of deeds,
a survey, God's plan,
a census of tribes seeking
a promised land. The end of the journey is fully described.
How it ended for Moses and the Israelites. Forty days
and forty nights of hardships and missteps,
errors made facing great wrath
as divine intervention
flared up on the righteous path.

No day was safe from grave
mistakes. For the beloved flock,
the strike of the rock ended the journey
before the promised revelation,
and sweet land of milk and honey
never was home for some.
A journey made, a chance for grace, gone.

My journey, all journeys, are deeply real,
internal and external - an intuitive feel.
I have found cause to march,
however harsh, a spiritual pilgrimage
to discover my transgressions,
murmurings and rebellions,
unlike the explorers of the Silk Road
seeking culture, language, yearning for gold,
trading spices, burnished saddles, hemp and rope.
My route is compassed to self discovery,
not materiality, but personal hope.

Is "here" always my destination?
Where is a sign, a manifestation?
Tibetan pilgrims carried brilliant swords,
with symbolic meaning and transformative words,
embellished with jewels pressed to scabbard and hilt,
elaborately decorated with mounts of gilt.
These blades of Wisdom cut through spiritual ignorance
for those with the courage to receive the subtle reflections.

Who am I? Where am I going? A universal call.
I ask it out loud, of one and of all.
I have always had a deep need for a guide,
a wise mentor by my side. Perhaps a spirit
with angels' wings, a crafty wizard's magic ring?
Or soul mates or seers to steer my way and
offer white gardenias as my pilgrim's bouquet.
Yet as I allow the unknown to enter
I may, alone, locate my center.

I find no map on ancient parchment,
no cryptic marks or symbols on wet
pavement. What I see in my minds eye are
black silver-flecked stones, pebbles of cloud grey
and flying high in the sky,
birds studded with diamonds
light my way.
One foot in front of the other
will follow the path... each step
purposed and navigated and
every cry, scream, misunderstanding, negotiated.
Quiet all agitation, fight ghostly demons,
wrestle with reenactments,
personas and histories redacted.

A wild tremor courses through me,
My heart pounds, my hands shake,
the ground, once so solid, begins to quake.
Accepting stasis prevents metamorphosis,
movement and change can be frightening
but heightens the senses like a bolt of lightening.
I acknowledge with gratitude the sadness and fear
bestowed upon me as life's canvas to create clarity.

In this journey is a moment of reckoning,
a covenant to myself and truth, a beckoning to
come to the end of the wilderness,
name my anger, resolve to awareness,
live life fully, woman, not object, savor
the hybrid I might be, embracing
citizenship with pride and dignity.

Pine Tree On Silk And A Yellow Linen Chair

And as if in a dream,
in the distance,
draped in its
cloak of misty blue,
the sun rises
from behind the clouds,
pine needles thread webs
of morning dew.

I sit at the kitchen table
on a yellow linen chair,
my heart tight, in tears,
the image blurred,
hands cold with fear
for my darling,
so ill, lying so still.
We fight for our love
and life. Hand upon
hand, we murmur brave
phrases, we enfold, we weep
with the tender joy
lovers have when they first meet.
Even as we caress,
gentle and sweet,
shivering, we stare,
aware of the danger,
as we try to sense
a future unknown.

Night falls, a tinted charcoal wash
bringing rest and calm.
Like the creatures brushed lightly on silk,
proud stag and his doe,
we awake to greet the milky dawn.
Blood pumping fiercely,
swift breath drawn, we are
trembling, vigilant, watching
for the slightest move.
Another day to embrace hope,
another day to love.

A Memory Of My Mother

Did I tell you I went to the
Beach last week?
The wind picked up mightily as I
Stepped out onto the hotel veranda
And the tall royal palm trees (so beloved in Florida)
that lined the courtyard
Lifted and bent their majestic fronds
As they whipped and wept in the west wind
With a sound like a thousand haystacks being thrown
Into the air

And, yes, that same week,
Oh!
The very next day
The wind dropped to a soft breeze as I
Stepped out onto the veranda
And the royal palms lining the courtyard
Graciously and gently dipped and bowed
Their crowns of pointed fronds
With a sound like a thousand mothers shushing their
Crying babes

And now the sea sparkles with dazzling pinpricks of light
Trembling across the surface of the undulating waves
Each and every sparkle sends
My heart and soul back to Cape Town
2012
To gaze upon another sea,
The vast Indian ocean rushing towards the tip of Africa,
While behind me,
Up a steep, shaded street,
In a small, sweet nursed clinic
My mother lay still on starched white sheets
And breathed less and less every day.
A sound like a thousand whispered goodbyes.

Breathe with me. Ubuntu

UBUNTU
I am the woman I am because of all women

UBUNTU
Our bodies as dust, in death, unite

UBUNTU
Your infant and mine suckle sweet swollen nippled milk

UBUNTU
The darkest night is followed by our shared dawn

UBUNTU
I do not share the color of your skin; but we are kindred

It's time to understand the strain,
the pain of racial hate,
listen with intention
and empathy
to stories of fear
and anxiety,
hear you pray
every day
that your boy or girl,
on the walk to school
with this recitation
reach their destination,
who understand
with comprehension
they could be stopped
by law enforcement
no rule broken,
just by birth,
young black children,
keep your head down,
hands in plain sight,
words unspoken.

Ubuntu!

Grant us,
with our safe white skins,
the right words to use.
Teach us how
to change the rules.
We associate but
do not appropriate,
leaving the legacy
of peace and equality,
to be your gift
to a nations' morality.

We, the people, alert in this moment,
600,000 remembered at Gettysburg,
brothers and cousins die on southern soil
for the emancipation proclamation
declaring slaves forever free
from the ruling Confederacy.
That was the promise
on January 1, 1863.

Yet some now take a knee
and bend their heads to pray
for a flag, star spangled, to
wave over America,
from sea to shining sea.
Each breath of your humanity
is mine too.
I am what I am because of you,
one with the dust
that is us.
UBUNTU

*Rev. Desmond Tutu
(Bantu language, South Africa)
*Ubuntu: "I am what I am because of who we all are"

Dance of the Crescent Moon

Heaven slumbers, silent, dark.
It's midnight and the melting clock
murmurs and measures the passage of time.
A deep decibel thunder-drum throbs
to the rhythmic stress of
hazy abstractions of talk,
punctuated pentameter of verse,
and violent verbs that fight to be heard
against the soulful sounds of a celestial sitar.
And between moon and earth,
Nataraja, cosmic dancer,
emerges, moving gracefully,
floating and meandering
through the anxious thoughts
and monologues of my mind.

The Doomsday dance calls forth Apasmara,
symbol of ignorance and sloth,
drifting through cataclysm and tragedy,
manna for perpetrators, political hacks
who deny and would fetter those who cry out,
voices as pure as the sound of the
rustle of the flames of transformation,
calling for sense and unity, a moment
to embrace moral and cultural community

The sound of the sitar moans
its moody calming notes, joined
by the sweet, silvery quaver of a flute.
Music swirls up to a crescent moon
draped in a cape of airy clouds,
where Nataraja beats the drum
of creation and star gods braid
bright botanicals into his hair;
he points downwards,
beckoning Apasmara
to join him in the evening dance,
to come to a reckoning for humanity,
a chance to face fate, life and death, create
a covenant of courtesy, ceremonial treaty.

Am I dreaming or dying as the last star disappears
and as, through my tears, I watch the sands of time slip
through the universe. I wait for a beginning or end,
untethered, as if in a trance,
never knowing with any certainty
when I will be part of the cosmic dance.

A Bird And The Hand

A sleek silhouetted hand reached across the land.
Pierced and pinched between skeletal fingers
she saw a fluttering of blue and gold feathers
and heard the thin clatter of a tiny bladed beak.
The wind slid, slipped and whipped around her room.
A gaudy summer dress flapped in distress.
A green glass bowl teetered at the edge of doom,
prophesying it's death of a thousand shards.

She floated towards the jewelled bird,
leaping onto a gazelle as blue as an old moon,
whose speed and soft brown eye, unerringly
carried her as Hera in her chariot,
toward the shadowed hand
that was obliterating her world.
But her wilderness protected her,
a reservoir of truth protected her,
courage coursed through her.
She would save the strange creature.

As she got closer she saw
the bliss of her soul enter the tiny bird,
it's feathers kissing her vermilion lips.
She watched it preen, stretch and release a strange
unearthly shriek as its peacock plumage
unfurled, a glowing fan of mystical beauty,
an ancient symbol of immortality,
unlocking the grip of the deathlike hand
weakened and limp, allowing her to breathe
and reconnect to life, even as she faced death.

Aah, the infinite sweetness of life,
the smallest of droplets of breath
fall like fine mist onto her damp pillow.
She smiled a small smile
and pulled her old blue and gold quilt
around her thin, quivering body, listening
to the sounds of an ordinary day.
The clinking of teacups; tinkling silver spoons,
the whistle of the kettle in the kitchen,
the bustling rustle of late afternoon.

She closed her eyes, allowed at last, a peaceful rest.
A single peacock feather drifted gently through the air
and, as if giving thanks, landed lovingly on her breast.

Again

I try to find sleep in my familiar bed,
a white cotton coverlet gently quilts around me,
but fear of the voices of nightmares fill my head
spitting hurtful words that fill me with dread.

Self-doubt in this dream is like a furnished room,
sofas stuffed and puffed with deadly words,
armchairs shaped alphabets spelling out faults,
starched pillows stitched with the meanest phrases
withhold softness that might comfort a sleeping child.
Ceilings soar fifty stories high,
trapping hope like a pale grey mote or frightened cry.
Cracked windows and walls slick with ancient grime,
punctuated by a door, locked, stuck for all time.

How can I silence voices wielding the weapon of words
to hurt, and demean and cut like a sword?
Can characters and tales, cartoons, and kind creatures
provide me with strategies and strong defences?
What did Humpty Dumpty say in a rather scornful tone,
"when I use a word it means just what I choose it to mean -
neither more nor less"
What about optimistic Alice who would make words mean
anything
With her innocence and a flounce of her apron and dress.
I hear the mordant voice of insecurity, small spirited and
mean,
ratcheting through my mind in this disturbing dream.
The sound is like the insistent caw of an evening crow
shocked at the sudden noise of the crack of a snapped twig.
And in the dark of a devils' goat night I thought I could run
through the dirt,
never look back, leave the braying sounds that forever hurt.
The insidious message, again and again,
speaks of betrayals of the past, hurt and pain,
and viciously predicts treasons that will last and last.

The adult reaches in to the child inside
holding her hand through time and locked doors
murmuring never say "can't " face the future and chant:
"see the truth, the blessing that is your life now"

The word blessing has an ancient connotation
For grace, love, sustenance, and avocation.
The sages offer the miracle of a word
as did Shakespeare in sonnets and George Bernard Shaw
who opined on the blessings of life, maybe more.
Lady Macbeth who " had most need of a blessing"
Emily Dickinson, sweet, startling poet,
writes "a word is dead, when it is said. Some say.
I say it just begins to live, that day"

A prison of hurt, a room with locked door
might hold no terrors for those who hold the key
of a mantra, a belief, a truth deep in their core.
words, like truth and beauty and life
said in prayer, or benediction, again and again,
as thought or a whisper can eliminate pain.
Even dreaming the meaning and acceptance of blessings,
Consecrates, sanctifies cruel rooms of depression
to become hallowed halls of trust and belief,
interior truth, beauty and life with space for relief
from the monotonous messages relayed through the brain,
towards the light of beauty, truth and life, again and again.

Leave the dark night and the caw of the crow.
Leave the dread rooms and their finials of doom.
Time has no power here - open the door,
step into the light, hold the hand of the child you once were.
Let go of the wrestling, the tangle of cruel words that cut like
swords,
find that place in your mind where again you can dance
with connection and redemption as you repeat the chant.

Once again the adult reaches in to the child inside
through time and locked doors,
holding hands, promising never to say "can't"
Whispering over and over, their special chant:
" see the truth and beauty that is your life now"

Bat

There are times when my breath is short,
I pump the bellows of my lungs, frantically
adding air to the heated sponge and calling
on the teachings of Master Nicklaus for elucidation
as to what would happen if my journey up the mountain
towards the dark cave of my destination,
would drown my soul or create a drought so
dry that the very vitality of my life—dust unto dust,
would wither and every lobe so perfect a host
for anger, love and peace,
then calm those very passions
would deny my heart its beat.

My purpose is strong, my temperament firm.
I feel a guardian protecting me from harm.
Although my soul's defences are weak and puny
surrounded by madness and massacres of Jews.
Yehudi, the word ricochets around the world,
reminding us we are human, Yehudi. Yehudi.
Jew means thankful.
But still I must reach the cave pushing uphill
through scrub and scabbed bush as if
forty days and forty nights must be endured,
by Pharaoh's orders, through roiling sun,
alone, for where will help come from?

I feel an onslaught—the depths of despair
bereft for six million plus eleven to add to the roster
of people who need
our care need our grief for centuries of prejudice
with no justice, redemption, or peace.
But what about the single heart, my heart,
who's shadowed
soul craves the inky black cave.
To hang upside down
in nature's sleep, not seeing the
funerals, pine boxes, and small bodies in white shrouds
or hearing the scrape of the shovel lift earthly mud
to lovingly begin the physical end
and begin a life of memory and pain.

I feel a slim cry, vibrating, ascending, at a pitch so high
it can only be heard by Adonai and I.
I find the God of the Caves who hears sacred prayers
from supplicants and applicants and bearers
of good luck mixed with tears.
Part bat, part human Camazotz rules his caves,
where I long to be safe in the belly of the earth,
letting go of these fears, preferring rebirth.
Bat hearts beating offering hope, dispelling dread,
emerging renewed each night, no myth of the dead.

I wish I was a bat with a millionfold community
to blot out the day, then, in total harmony,
as the day ends and all, as one,
swoop out to greet the setting sun.

Memory Fragments

With a wistful gaze I stare out my window,
mourning the loss of a sweet beloved.

*Emily's words float through my mind

" I cannot live with You –
It would be Life –
And Life is over there –
Behind the Shelf
Discarded of the Housewife –
Quaint – or Broke –
A newer Sevres pleases –
Old Ones crack – "
A valley of folded green hills is bathed
in the late sunshine of the day.
My mind slips back in time.

Memories so set, so definite,
so bright, now come to me
as rivers of light or spiral me
into frightening dark corners
I would rather forget.

I can summon moments
of a fragrance, a texture,
remnants of conversations,
the most tender proclamations of love,
the shrillest declarations
of hate and hurt. These are all
fragments, precious to me, even so.

So much is forgotten, but the
moment of meeting my first love
lies warm within me. A student,
just a boy, slim, blue black hair, soft beard
and intelligent, flirtatious green eyes.
I remember that shock of recognition,
an electric shock that went through
me and changed me forever.

A first dance, my cheek rubbing
against his rough tweed jacket,
the perfume of sandalwood, pungent
musk, wrapped around me. I folded into him, feeling
like the folds of the hills slipping into dusk.

Bright winter afternoon, icy cold.
We sit in an enclosed sunny porch.
He played the guitar. He gently
stroked my hair, softly kissed me,
caressed me, held me, and time
stood still, suspended, as if
we could be like this forever.

And yet, even then, my darling
first love hurt me, lacerated my
soul, punctured my love,
still I did not leave.
With the precision of someone who
did not care, he looked coldly
at my face, drenched with tears.
And when I begged him to stay,
to remember the years of passion,
for our love to be strong,
he turned, his back rigid
with indifference, he left the room.

I want to embrace these thoughts, these
tender memories. The ugly hurts, like a twist of a knife,
are evidence of the essence of a life.
Remembrances tint the passage of time,
the colors of memories that
make up the puzzle. The picture is almost
visible. One empty spot, right in the middle.

*Emily Dickinson, poet 1830-1886.

A Hot Afternoon In Nice

It was a hot afternoon in Nice.
Twenty four hours ago I was in London,
seething and hurt, emotions as rumpled as my bed.
The beach was stacked with rows of red
striped deck chairs (property of La Mer Grande Hotel),
that seen from above, appeared as a large undulating flag.
Umbrellas popped up and were soon
festooned with gaudy beach towels
creating a sort of strange Bedouin camp,
an oasis for exhausted tourists, nannies,
children and small poodles.

I sat in a section with plain canvas deck chairs near the pier,
where the desultory waves of the Mediterranean
slapped around the beams with rather murky abandon,
and the shadows were so deep no umbrellas were called for.

From our small flat in London
I imagined you here studying sun drenched buildings,
the architecture of light and the textures
of the blue windows of the tiny chapel at Vence.
Partly proud, and a bit jealous of your Matisse moment
I phoned the hostel one morning.
I phoned the hostel that afternoon and again at 11pm.
Madame did not know where you were. Desole.

I boarded the flight to Nice the next morning.
It was July 1969. We were nineteen, passionate
and often afraid of the wildness of our obsessions.

I waited and watched for you from the shadows,
trying to stay on message. Where were you every day
and every night? Do I want to know?
I am so cold yet the heat, just a few feet away,
shimmers, boils. I don't
take my eyes off the hot boardwalk.
You don't see me, but at last I see you
as large and clear as an Henri cut-out,
walking with a laughing, dark haired
girl. So confident, free, so unaware of the
gigantic hurt blocking the sun.
I stare, willing you to look up
as if the sheer force of my
love could communicate across the sands.
Our eyes meet. You are confused, unsure.
I might be a ghost, an apparition.
These things happen. The girl looks at me.
She nods to him and quickly walks off. I stand,
taking short, sharp breaths that merge with yours.
You take me in your arms.
The umbrellas gleamed red, the sky mashed blue
and a shaft of sunlight reached under the pier,
creating the red and purple prisms of a Matisse interior,
the dappled patterns of his Moorish floors.

I love you.

Without speaking we went to the hostel.
I saw the old black phone in the hall. I heard,
from the gloom of the canteen, the sound of
Bob Dylan singing Lay Lady Lay.
We made love in your small room,
that afternoon in Nice.

Roses

The air was warm that day in Golders Green,
unseasonably, but the windows
were open to catch the meek breeze,
and we could easily see bright red buses
flashing by on the way to the city,
number 13 and number 460,
packed with schoolgirls avidly tapping on phones
while ladies in grey knitted cardigans, made their way home.

She sat on the white couch,
plumped pillows billowed around.
We talked about the roses outside,
how their perfume was so intense
in these warm, late summer days.
Their colors of rich yellow,
sweet pinks, the velvet reds seem
different this year, maybe we're just older,
we said, or maybe London used to be colder.

She nodded and smiled,
prepared to pour tea,
offer warm scones, strawberry jam and cream.
Light filtered in, dust motes danced.
All seemed so peaceful until she remarked
that the roses were lovely this year don't we think?
Their yellows, deep reds and heavenly pinks.

She talked about her late husband,
their days of parties, nightclubs, laughter,
not recognizing I was his daughter.
I thought I knew, I thought I would understand,
now I have no pretensions,
I felt shock, disbelief when faced with dementia.
How do you love, care or be kind, I thought,
when your memories that guide, fail, you are lost.
In brief spells of clarity, reason and lucidity,
you know in an instant you are unable to summon
the joys and the sorrows of life's changing story.

It's harrowing to watch someone desperate
To connect, to locate the center of that we forget.
To articulate memories from decades or seconds ago,
fragmented, off center, places, people, events
recalled dimly and partially shredded,
seen through a prism the brain has constructed.

You see in their eyes a glimmer of strain
to recall and remain in the present,
gazing at faded photos, their
static images staring out, willing a memory.
No frisson of recognition or flutter of lids indicates
anything but a faint, anxious look; the conversation
lulls so we smile reassuringly, snap photos and pose,
and continue to praise the late summer rose.

Covenant Compass

You are trying to hold back tears.

You are afraid of being afraid
Boundaries buckle, tides suck back into moonlit shoals

Your eyes are as dry as Venus. A single lash snaps.

You are lost. Your compass has no North
The shadowed sea becomes red with an eastern sun

Your face bubbles with salt and foam

and freezes in the ice flows of the south
milk sap in your bloated breast, gently floats you to the West

You arch your back over chasms and mountains.

your hand reaches
your lips speak
no fathomless fate
at the mercy of the
serpent of Genesis
persuades your journey
Free will guides your compass
to the gleamed west sunset shards
towards acceptance and peace
closer to a faraway God